Night Before Christmas

by Paula Masters
Illustrated by Zoey Masters

*Dedicated to my twinkling stars,
Grace, Aliyah, Maxwell, Charlie, Auggie, Oli, Vanny,
Henry, Essie, Gabby, and Arthur.*

'Twas the night before Christmas
with no room at the Inn.

A small, drafty barn
is where our story begins.

Mary had readied the manger with care—

made a cozy small crib for the babe she would bear.

The wise men were nestled
all snug in their beds,

while visions of starry skies
danced in their heads.

But Mary in her labor,
and Joseph by her side,

were eagerly awaiting
their baby's first cry.

They huddled together—
wondered what this could mean—
with their eyes they beheld
an astonishing scene.

The angels each robed
  with the glory of God—

filled the shepherds with fear,
  left them silent and awed.

Up high in the clouds,
  the heralds were voicing,

all praise to the Lord,
  with wild rejoicing.

More rapid than eagles
  His cherubs they came,

singing, "Glory to God,"
  and exalting Christ's name.

In song after song,
  of good will and of favor—

the chorus announced
  good news of the Savior.

"Now shepherds, now wise men,
 now children and nurses;

come wealthy, come bankrupt,
 come kings with your purses."

And then, in a twinkling,
 the angels were gone.

Taking hold of their staffs,
 the shepherds moved on.

They collected their sheep,
 and headed to town,

to welcome the Christ child,
 where he could be found.

He was swaddled in cloths,
  and so peaceful he lay—

all snuggled up warm
  in a trough full of hay.

Three wise men were there,
  bowing down to this lamb.

They'd come a great distance
  to find the "I AM."

The shepherds arrived
   with praises to sing,

lyrics of angels
   for the new born king.

The closer they got,
   the weaker their knees,

but his gurgles and coos
   put them softly at ease.

The legs of the manger
   held him steady beneath,

while the creatures encircled
   his head like a wreath.

A bundle of gifts
   were laid at his feet—

gold and myrrh,
   and frankincense sweet.

His eyes—how they twinkled!
 His dimples how merry!

His cheeks were like roses,
 his nose like a cherry!

His droll little mouth
 was drawn up like a bow,

and they gazed at his majesty
 beneath the moon's glow.

This was the moment
 they knew deep within,

the child was the answer
 to all the world's sin.

They'd heard from the scriptures
 the story that told

of a prince who would rescue
 the young and the old.

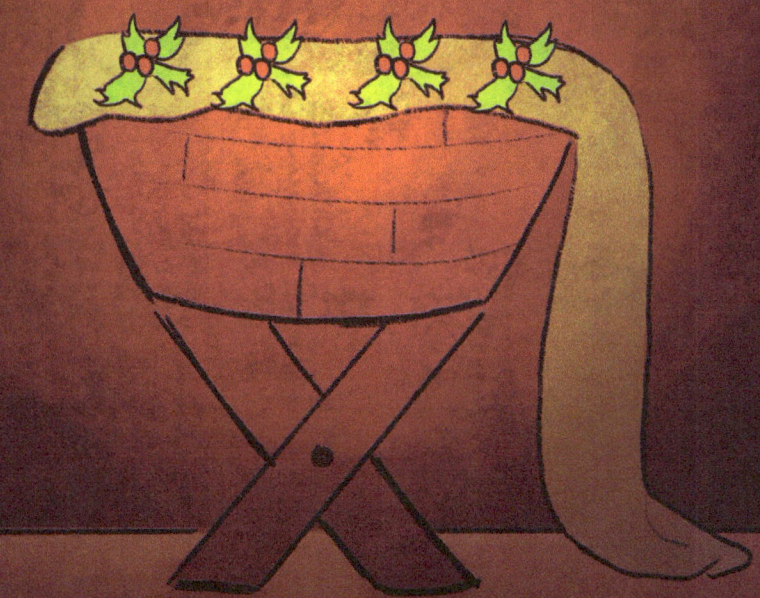

God's gift to his people,
 a very great treasure,

came down from heaven,
 with worth beyond measure.

And this is a gift
   that God is still giving:

hope to the heart
   where Christ is now living.

Christmas shines still,
 just as brightly today.

The Savior has come;
 we rejoice in this way:

there are presents and ribbons
and shiny red bows,

with stockings and garlands
all hung in straight rows.

And the house is warm
and our family is near,

and our hearts are filled
with love and good cheer,

Author Paula Masters created *Night Before Christmas* as a way to remind readers of all ages that they are part of something strikingly uncommon—something magnificently otherworldly! Paula has also authored *Blue Skies: Beyond The Dark Clouds Of Broken Thinking*, as well as, *Exceptional Bloom: Coming Alive After Fifty*. Paula is married to her husband Jeff and lives in South Florida. They have five adult daughters and 11 grandchildren.

Illustrator Zoey Masters, the youngest daughter of Paula and Jeff, lives in Orlando where she spends her time creating timeless illustrations. She enjoys showcasing her art at Comic Conventions while cosplaying her characters in real-time. Zoey is currently working on an exciting comic novel.

www.ingramcontent.com/pod-product-compliance
Lightning Source LLC
Chambersburg PA
CBHW040738150426
42811CB00064B/1781